INDIAN HANDICRAFTS

A CULTURAL EXPLORATION OF THE CRAFTS AND TEXTILE TRADITIONS OF INDIA

DR. JAGADEESH PILLAI

Made with ♥ on the Notion Press Platform
www.notionpress.com

|| "Dedicated to all who seek to understand and appreciate Indian culture and tradition." ||

ᘓ

Contents

Contents

PRAYER

"Om Bhadram Karnebhih Shrunuyaama DevaahBhadram Pashyemaakshabhiryajatraah SthirairangaistushtuvaamsastanoobhihVyashema Devahitam YadaayuhSwasti Na Indro VridhashravaahSwasti Nah Pooshaa VishwavedaahSwasti Nastaarkshyo ArishtanemihSwasti No Brihaspatir DadhaatuOm Shantih, Shantih, Shantih"

The literal meaning of this mantra is: OM. O Gods! Let us hear auspicious words from our ears. O reverent Gods! Let us behold propitious visions from our eyes, let our organs and body be stable, healthy, and strong. Let us do that which is pleasing to the gods in the life span allotted to us. May Indra, inscribed in the scriptures, bring us fortune! May Pushan, the knower of the world, grant us prosperity! May Trakshya, who vanquishes enemies, bestow us with blessings! May Brihaspati bring us success!
OM Peace, Peace, Peace.

About The Author

Dr. Jagadeesh Pillai is a renowned Guinness World Record holder, writer, and researcher hailing from Varanasi, also known as the abode of Lord Shiva. With a Ph.D. in Vedic Science and a range of creative ideas and achievements, he is a true polymath. He is the author of more than 100 books including Research Publications. Although his roots can be traced back to Kerala, the people of Varanasi hold him in high regard and affectionately consider him one of their own.

Dr. Pillai has achieved four Guinness World Records in the following subjects:

"Script to Screen" - In this record, Dr. Pillai produced and directed an animation film within the shortest time possible, breaking the previous record set by Canadians. He has also received numerous national and international awards and recognitions for this achievement.

Longest Line of Postcards - For this record, Dr. Pillai created a line of 16,300 postcards on the occasion of the 163rd anniversary of Indian Postal Day. The event also included a questionnaire about the Indian flag.

Largest Poster Awareness Campaign - Dr. Pillai designed an awareness campaign on the subject of "Beti Bachao - Beti Padhao" (Save the Girl Child - Educate the Girl Child) to achieve this record.

Largest Envelope - In tribute to the Indian Prime Minister's

"Make in India" initiative, Dr. Pillai created a 4000 square meter envelope using waste paper to achieve this record.

Attempted - **70000 Candles on a 210 kg Cake** - To celebrate the 70th Indian Independence Day, Dr. Pillai attempted to light 70,000 candles on a 210 kg cake, which was recorded in World Records India.

Attempted - **Documentary on Dhamek Stupa of Sarnath in 17 Languages** - Dr. Pillai attempted to create a documentary on the Dhamek Stupa of Sarnath, dubbing it in 17 different languages. The result of this attempt is currently awaiting confirmation from the Guinness World Records.

Dr. Pillai is skilled in teaching the Bhagavad Gita, a Hindu scripture, and is popular among young people. He has helped many young people improve their lives through his motivational teachings.

In addition to teaching, he has composed and sung numerous Sanskrit Bhajans and patriotic songs.

He has also written and directed several short films and documentaries for awareness campaigns, and has volunteered with the police in both UP and Kerala to spread awareness about various issues through videos and photography.

Incredibly, he has produced and directed over 100 documentaries about the city of Varanasi, all on his own.

He has also helped and guided more than 25 boys and girls to achieve world records through creative and innovative methods. He is a multifaceted person who uses his intellect and the blessings given to him by God to excel in various areas. He is both a teacher and a student, always learning and teaching, and is able to master any subject he comes across.

He is a selfless social activist and motivational speaker who has overcome struggles and failures to become a successful and enthusiastic individual with a rich life experience.

In addition to his work with the Bhagavad Gita, he is also an efficient Tarot card reader, Astro-Vastu consultant, and a talented singer and composer. He has sung the entire Ram Charita Manas and Bhagavad Gita in his own compositions, and has sung the phrase "Lokah Samastha Sukhino Bhavantu" in 50 different languages. He is currently working on a detailed and scientific study of Vedas, Upanishads, Puranas, and the Bhagavad Gita. He has also composed and sung the Hanuman Chalisa and Gayatri Mantra in 108 and 1008 different compositions, respectively.

Awards - Four Times Guinness World Records, Winner of Mahatma Gandhi Vishwa Shanti Puraskar, Mahatma Gandhi Global Peace Ambassador, Kashi Ratna Award, Dr. APJ Abdul Kalam Motivational Person of the Year 2017, Mother Teresa Award, Indira Gandhi Priyadarshini Award, Bharat Vikas Ratna Award, Udyog Ratna Award, Vigyan Prasar Award, Poorvanchal Ratn Samman.

PREFACE

The book "Indian Handicrafts: A Cultural Exploration of the Crafts and Textile Traditions of India" is a comprehensive guide to the rich and diverse world of Indian handicrafts. From traditional textile making techniques to contemporary designs, this book delves into the history, significance, and ongoing relevance of Indian handicrafts.

The book begins with an introduction to the evolution of Indian handicrafts, providing a historical overview of the various crafts and textile traditions of the country. It then goes on to explore the different types of handicrafts in India, including embroidery, block printing, pottery and ceramics, metal crafts, wood crafts, jewelry and accessory making, and leather crafts.

In addition, the book also covers the folk and tribal arts of India, as well as the role of handicrafts in Indian society and culture. The book also delves into the contemporary Indian handicrafts and design, and the impact of the export of Indian handicrafts. It concludes with a discussion on the conservation and revival of Indian handicrafts.

This book is an invaluable resource for anyone interested in learning more about Indian handicrafts, their history, and significance. It is also useful for artisans, designers, researchers, and students of Indian culture and heritage. It is written with the aim of providing an in-depth understanding of the diversity, richness and the cultural heritage of Indian handicrafts, as well as their ongoing relevance and importance in today's world.

I

Introduction: The Evolution of Indian Handicrafts

The art of Indian handicrafts has a rich and vibrant history that dates back to ancient times. From intricate hand-woven textiles to hand-carved woodwork, Indian handicrafts have evolved over the centuries to become a defining aspect of the country's cultural heritage.

In ancient India, handicrafts were not just a means of creating functional objects, but also a way of expressing cultural and religious beliefs. From the intricate stone carvings of the Indus Valley Civilization to the beautifully crafted bronze statues of the Chola Dynasty, ancient Indian handicrafts were a reflection of the country's rich cultural heritage.

As the country evolved, so too did its handicrafts. During

the Mughal period, Indian handicrafts reached new heights of refinement and sophistication. The Mughals were great patrons of the arts and their influence can be seen in the intricate designs and delicate craftsmanship of Indian textiles, jewelry, and metalwork from this period.

The British colonial period had a major impact on Indian handicrafts. With the advent of industrialization, traditional handicrafts faced competition from mass-produced goods. However, during this period, Indian handicrafts also found new markets and audience in the West, where they were highly sought after for their unique and intricate designs.

After independence, the Indian government has taken several steps to preserve and promote the country's rich handicraft heritage. The establishment of organizations like the Central Cottage Industries Corporation and the National Handicrafts and Handlooms Museum helped to revive and promote traditional crafts. Today, Indian handicrafts are exported to countries around the world and are highly valued for their unique designs and traditional craftsmanship.

In recent years, there has been a renewed interest in Indian handicrafts, both within the country and abroad. This renewed interest is driven by a desire to connect with traditional culture and a growing awareness of the environmental and social benefits of supporting local crafts.

Indian Handicrafts have been an integral part of the country's cultural heritage. From ancient times to the present day, these crafts have evolved and adapted to changing times, while maintaining their unique designs and traditional craftsmanship. Today, Indian Handicrafts are highly valued and sought after for their beauty and cultural significance, and efforts are being made to preserve and promote these crafts for future generations to enjoy.

It's important to note that Indian Handicrafts are not just limited to certain regions but are found all over India, each region has its own specialty, like the Banarasi silk from Varanasi, the Blue Pottery from Jaipur, the Pashmina shawls from Kashmir, the Chikankari from Lucknow, the Kantha from West Bengal and many more. Each of these crafts has its own story to tell, and each one is a reflection of the rich cultural heritage of India.

"Handicrafts are not a luxury, but a necessity for preserving the cultural heritage of a nation."

- Mahatma Gandhi

☙

II

Traditional Textile Making Techniques in India

India has a rich history of textile making, dating back to ancient times. Traditional textile making techniques in India include hand-weaving, block printing, tie-dye, and embroidery. Each technique has its own unique characteristics and is associated with different regions of the country.

Hand-weaving is one of the oldest textile making techniques in India and is still widely practiced today. Hand-woven fabrics are known for their durability, texture, and intricate designs. Different regions in India have their own unique hand-weaving techniques and styles, such as the Banarasi silk from Varanasi, the Kanchipuram silk from Tamil Nadu, and the Paithani silk from Maharashtra.

Block printing is another traditional textile making technique in India. It involves using wooden blocks to print designs on fabric. The blocks are carved with the desired design and then dipped in dye. The fabric is then pressed against the block, transferring the design onto the fabric. Block printing is particularly associated with the state of Rajasthan, where it has a long history and is still widely practiced today.

Tie-dye, also known as bandhani, is a traditional textile making technique found in Gujarat and Rajasthan. It involves tying small knots in the fabric before dyeing it. The tied areas of the fabric resist the dye, creating intricate patterns on the fabric.

Embroidery is another traditional textile making technique in India. It is associated with different regions of the country, such as the Chikankari from Lucknow, the Zardozi from Uttar Pradesh and the Kashida from Kashmir. Embroidery is a highly skilled craft that involves decorating fabric with needle and thread. The designs can be simple or intricate and are often inspired by nature or traditional motifs.

In conclusion, Traditional textile making techniques in India are vast and varied. Each technique has its own unique characteristics, and is associated with different regions of the country. From hand-weaving to block printing, tie-dye, and embroidery, these traditional techniques are still widely practiced today and are an important part of India's cultural heritage.

"The art of India is the art of living."

- Ananda Coomaraswamy

ல

III

The Embroidery Traditions of India

Embroidery is an ancient and traditional textile making technique in India that has a rich history and cultural significance. Different regions in India have their own unique embroidery traditions, each with their own techniques, styles, and motifs.

One of the most famous traditional embroidery techniques in India is the Chikankari from Lucknow, Uttar Pradesh. Chikankari is a type of white-on-white embroidery that is traditionally done on muslin and other lightweight fabrics. The designs are typically floral and geometric patterns and the technique is known for its delicate and intricate work.

Another traditional embroidery tradition in India is the Zardozi from Uttar Pradesh. Zardozi is a type of metal thread embroidery that is typically done on silk and velvet fabrics. The designs are often elaborate and heavily embellished, and the technique is known for its opulence and grandeur.

The Kantha from West Bengal is another ancient embroidery tradition of India. It's a simple running stitch that is used to create motifs, patterns and designs. It's often done on old saris and dhotis, the resulting fabric is then used to make quilts, cushion covers, and other home decor items.

The Kashida from Kashmir is known for its fine and delicate needlework, it's done on Pashmina shawls and other woolen fabrics. The motifs used are typically inspired by nature, such as flowers, leaves, and birds.

The Phulkari from Punjab is another traditional embroidery tradition of India, it's done on cotton and silk fabrics with the use of brightly colored silk floss. The designs are typically large and bold, featuring geometric shapes and floral motifs.

The embroidery traditions of India are diverse and varied. Each tradition has its own unique techniques, styles, and motifs, and is associated with different regions of the country. From Chikankari to Zardozi, Kantha, Kashida, Phulkari, these traditional embroidery techniques are an important part of India's cultural heritage and are still widely practiced today. These embroidery techniques are not only a way to adorn fabrics but also a way to preserve and pass on cultural heritage from one generation to another.

"Handicrafts are the embodiment of the cultural heritage of a nation and an expression of the creative genius of its people."

- Narendra Modi

ॐ

IV

Block Printing in India: Techniques and Styles

Block printing is a traditional textile making technique in India that has a long history and rich cultural significance. The technique involves using carved wooden blocks to print designs on fabric. The blocks are dipped in dye, and then pressed onto the fabric to transfer the design. The technique is widely practiced in the state of Rajasthan and other regions in India.

The traditional block printing techniques in India are mainly divided into two categories: hand block printing and machine block printing.

Hand block printing is the most traditional and time-honored technique. It is a labor-intensive process that involves carving the design into the wooden block by hand,

and then printing it onto the fabric by hand. This technique allows for greater flexibility and creativity in terms of design, and the resulting prints are known for their intricate detail and vibrant colors.

Machine block printing is a more recent technique that involves using a printing machine to transfer the design onto the fabric. This method is faster and more efficient than hand block printing, but it is less flexible in terms of design. Machine printed fabrics are known for their consistency and uniformity, but the designs may not be as intricate or detailed as those created with hand block printing.

In terms of styles, there are many different styles of block printing in India, each with its own unique characteristics. The Ajrakh from Kutch, Gujarat is known for its bold geometric patterns and use of natural dyes. The Bagru from Rajasthan is known for its use of simple, bold designs and bright colors. The Dabu from Rajasthan is a mud resist printing technique, known for its earthy tones and rustic feel. The Kalamkari from Andhra Pradesh is known for its fine details and use of vegetable dyes.

Block printing is a traditional textile making technique in India that has a long history and rich cultural significance. The technique is widely practiced in the state of Rajasthan and other regions in India. The traditional block printing techniques in India are mainly divided into two categories: hand block printing and machine block printing. Each region and style of block printing has its own unique characteristics and the resulting prints are known for their intricate designs, vibrant colors and cultural significance.

"Handicrafts are the true wealth of a nation, as they represent the culture and traditions of a people."

- Rabindranath Tagore

ꞷ

V

Traditional Pottery and Ceramics in India

India has a rich history of traditional pottery and ceramics dating back to ancient times. Different regions in India have their own unique pottery and ceramics traditions, each with their own techniques, styles, and motifs.

One of the most famous traditional pottery and ceramics techniques in India is the Blue Pottery from Jaipur, Rajasthan. Blue Pottery is a type of pottery that is glazed using a special blue dye and decorated with intricate designs. The technique is known for its delicate and intricate work and is often used to create vases, bowls, and other decorative items.

The traditional pottery of the Harappan civilization, which dates back to around 2600 BCE, is another ancient pottery tradition in India. The Harappan pottery was known for its high quality, and was used to create a wide range of functional and decorative items.

The traditional pottery of the Black and Red Ware culture, which dates back to around 2000 BCE, is another ancient pottery tradition in India. The Black and Red Ware pottery was known for its fine quality and was used to create a wide range of functional and decorative items.

The traditional pottery of the Ahar culture, which dates back to around 2000 BCE is another ancient pottery tradition of India. The Ahar pottery was known for its fine quality and was used to create a wide range of functional and decorative items.

The traditional pottery of the Gray Ware culture, which dates back to around 2000 BCE, is another ancient pottery tradition in India. The Gray Ware pottery was known for its fine quality and was used to create a wide range of functional and decorative items.

Traditional pottery and ceramics in India have a rich history and cultural significance. Different regions in India have their own unique pottery and ceramics traditions, each with their own techniques, styles, and motifs. From the Blue Pottery of Jaipur to the ancient pottery of Harappan, Black and Red Ware, Ahar, Gray Ware culture, these traditional techniques are an important part of India's cultural heritage and are still widely practiced today. These pottery and ceramics techniques not only serve functional purposes but also have aesthetic and cultural values.

ॐ

"The beauty of Indian art and craft lies in its simplicity, elegance, and the way it reflects the country's rich culture and heritage."

- L.K. Advani

ꕤ

VI

The Metal Crafts of India

Metal craft is an ancient and traditional craft in India that has a rich history and cultural significance. Different regions in India have their own unique metal crafts traditions, each with their own techniques, styles, and motifs.

One of the most famous traditional metal crafts in India is the bronze casting from the state of Tamil Nadu. This technique is known for its intricate and detailed sculptures, mainly of Hindu gods and goddesses. The sculptures are made by the process of lost-wax casting, which involves creating a wax model of the sculpture, which is then covered in clay and heated to remove the wax and harden the clay. The resulting mold is then filled with molten bronze, creating the final sculpture.

The traditional metal craft of the Bidriware from the state

of Karnataka is another famous metal craft in India. The technique involves creating intricate designs on the surface of a zinc alloy using a silver inlay technique. The craft is known for its intricate designs and the use of bold geometric patterns.

The traditional metal craft of the Dhokra from the state of West Bengal is another ancient metal craft in India. This technique is known for its use of the lost-wax casting method and for its intricate designs and detailed figurines.

The traditional metal craft of the Bell metal from the state of Odisha is another ancient metal craft in India. This technique is known for its use of the lost-wax casting method and for its intricate designs and detailed figurines.

The traditional metal craft of the Brassware from the state of Uttar Pradesh is another ancient metal craft in India. This technique is known for its intricate designs and detailed figurines, mainly used for home decor and functional items.

The metal crafts of India have a rich history and cultural significance. Different regions in India have their own unique metal crafts traditions, each with their own techniques, styles, and motifs. From the bronze casting of Tamil Nadu to the Bidriware of KarnATAKA, Dhokra of West Bengal, Bell metal of Odisha and Brassware of Uttar Pradesh, these traditional metal crafts are an important part of India's cultural heritage and are still widely practiced today. These metal crafts not only serve functional purposes but also have aesthetic and cultural values.

"Indian traditional art and craft is an integral part of the country's cultural heritage and must be protected and promoted for future generations to enjoy."

- Sushma Swaraj

ജ

VII

The Wood Crafts of India

India has a rich history of woodcraft, dating back to ancient times. Different regions in India have their own unique woodcraft traditions, each with their own techniques, styles, and motifs.

One of the most famous traditional woodcraft techniques in India is the rosewood carving from the state of Andhra Pradesh. Rosewood is a fragrant hardwood that is known for its durability and rich, dark color. The rosewood carvings are typically intricate and detailed, and are often used to create decorative items such as furniture, statues, and household items.

The traditional woodcraft of the Sandalwood from the state of Karnataka is another famous woodcraft in India. The Sandalwood is a fragrant hardwood that is known for its durability and rich, dark color. The Sandalwood carvings are typically intricate and detailed, and are often used to create decorative items such as statues, furniture, and household items.

The traditional woodcraft of the Teak from the state of Tamil Nadu is another ancient woodcraft in India. The teak is a strong and durable hardwood that is known for its resistance to rot and decay. The teak carvings are typically intricate and detailed and are often used to create decorative items such as furniture, statues, and household items.

The traditional woodcraft of the Jackfruit from the state of West Bengal is another ancient woodcraft in India. The Jackfruit tree is known for its durability and resistance to rot and decay. The Jackfruit carvings are typically intricate and detailed and are often used to create decorative items such as furniture, statues, and household items.

The woodcrafts of India have a rich history and cultural significance. Different regions in India have their own unique woodcraft traditions, each with their own techniques, styles, and motifs. From the rosewood carving of Andhra Pradesh to the Sandalwood of KarnATAKA, Teak of Tamil Nadu and Jackfruit of West Bengal, these traditional woodcrafts are an important part of India's cultural heritage and are still widely practiced today. These woodcrafts not only serve functional purposes but also have aesthetic and cultural values.

"Handicrafts are not only a means of livelihood for the artisans, but also a way of preserving India's rich cultural heritage."

- Smriti Irani

ꕥ

VIII

The Jewelry and Accessory making traditions of India

India has a rich history of jewelry and accessory making, dating back to ancient times. Different regions in India have their own unique jewelry and accessory making traditions, each with their own techniques, styles, and motifs.

One of the most famous traditional jewelry and accessory making techniques in India is the gold and diamond jewelry making from the state of Gujarat. This technique is known for its intricate and detailed designs, often featuring elaborate floral patterns and motifs.

The traditional jewelry and accessory making of the Meenakari from the state of Rajasthan is another famous tradition in India. Meenakari is a type of enameling that is used to decorate gold and silver jewelry. The technique involves applying layers of colored enamel to the metal surface, which is then engraved with intricate designs. The craft is known for its bright and vibrant colors and intricate designs.

The traditional jewelry and accessory making of the Kundan from the state of Rajasthan is another ancient tradition in India. Kundan is a type of jewelry that is made by setting precious stones, such as diamonds and emeralds, into a gold base. The craft is known for its intricate designs and the use of high-quality precious stones.

The traditional jewelry and accessory making of the Temple jewelry from the state of Tamil Nadu is another ancient tradition in India. Temple jewelry is a type of jewelry that is used to adorn the gods and goddesses in Hindu temples. The craft is known for its intricate designs and the use of high-quality precious stones.

The jewelry and accessory making traditions of India have a rich history and cultural significance. Different regions in India have their own unique traditions, each with their own techniques, styles, and motifs. From the gold and diamond jewelry making of Gujarat to the Meenakari of Rajasthan, Kundan of Rajasthan and Temple jewelry of Tamil Nadu, these traditional crafts are an important part of India's cultural heritage and are still widely practiced today. These jewelry and accessory making traditions not only serve functional purposes but also have aesthetic and cultural values.

"Indian traditional art and craft is a reflection of the country's rich diversity, and it is our duty to preserve and promote it."

- Manmohan Singh

ꙮ

IX

The traditional leather crafts of India

India has a rich history of traditional leather crafts, dating back to ancient times. Different regions in India have their own unique leather craft traditions, each with their own techniques, styles, and motifs.

One of the most famous traditional leather crafts in India is the Jutefootwear from the state of Uttar Pradesh. Jute is a natural vegetable fiber that is known for its durability, and Jutefootwear is made from Jute fibers and is comfortable and eco-friendly. The footwear is typically decorated with intricate designs and motifs.

The traditional leather crafts of the Mojari from the state of Rajasthan is another famous tradition in India. The Mojari is a type of traditional footwear made of leather and is decorated with intricate embroidery and embellishments. The craft is known for its comfort and durability.

The traditional leather crafts of the Kappawork from the state of Tamil Nadu is another ancient tradition in India. The Kappawork is a type of traditional footwear made of leather and is decorated with intricate embroidery and embellishments. The craft is known for its comfort and durability.

The traditional leather crafts of the Chappal from the state of West Bengal is another ancient tradition in India. The Chappal is a type of traditional footwear made of leather and is decorated with intricate embroidery and embellishments. The craft is known for its comfort and durability.

The traditional leather crafts of India have a rich history and cultural significance. Different regions in India have their own unique traditions, each with their own techniques, styles, and motifs. From the Jutefootwear of Uttar Pradesh to the Mojari of Rajasthan, Kappawork of Tamil Nadu, and Chappal of West Bengal, these traditional leather crafts are an important part of India's cultural heritage and are still widely practiced today. These leather crafts not only serve functional purposes but also have aesthetic and cultural values.

"Handicrafts are the soul of India, they reflect the country's rich culture, heritage and traditions."

- Pranab Mukherjee

X

Folk and tribal arts in India

India is home to a diverse range of folk and tribal art forms, each with their own unique styles, techniques, and motifs. These art forms are deeply rooted in the cultural heritage of the communities that create them and are often passed down through generations.

One of the most famous folk art forms in India is the Warli art from the state of Maharashtra. Warli art is a type of tribal art that is characterized by simple geometric shapes and motifs. It is traditionally created using a mixture of rice paste and water on mud walls, and is used to depict scenes from daily life, such as farming and rituals.

The Madhubani art form from the state of Bihar is another famous folk art in India. This art form is known for its bright colors and bold lines, and it is typically used to depict scenes from Hindu mythology and daily life. The technique involves using a variety of tools, including fingers, twigs, and matchsticks, to apply the paint to the surface.

The Pattachitra art form from the state of Odisha is another ancient folk art in India. This art form is known for its intricate and detailed paintings, which are typically done on cloth or palm leaf and depict scenes from Hindu mythology. The technique involves using natural dyes and pigments to create the vibrant colors.

The Gond art form from the state of Madhya Pradesh is another ancient folk art in India. This art form is known for its bold and colorful paintings, which are typically done on walls, fabrics, and paper. The technique involves using natural dyes and pigments to create the vibrant colors.

India is home to a diverse range of folk and tribal art forms, each with their own unique styles, techniques, and motifs. These art forms are deeply rooted in the cultural heritage of the communities that create them and are often passed down through generations. From Warli art of Maharashtra to Madhubani art of Bihar, Pattachitra of Odisha, Gond art of Madhya Pradesh, these traditional art forms are an important part of India's cultural heritage and continue to be widely practiced today. These art forms not only serve functional purposes but also have aesthetic and cultural values.

"Handicrafts are not only a means of livelihood for artisans, but also an expression of the country's rich cultural heritage and diversity."

- Nitin Gadkari

&

XI

The role of Handicrafts in Indian society and culture

Handicrafts have played a significant role in Indian society and culture for centuries. They are an important part of India's cultural heritage and are deeply rooted in the country's rich history and traditions.

Handicrafts have played a major role in preserving and promoting Indian culture and heritage. They are an expression of the country's diverse cultural, ethnic, and regional identities and are a reflection of the lifestyle, customs, and traditions of the communities that create them. Handicrafts are also a medium of storytelling, depicting the myths, legends, and daily life of the people.

Handicrafts also play a significant economic role in India. They provide employment opportunities for a large number of people, particularly in rural and remote areas, where traditional crafts are an important source of livelihood. They also contribute to the country's economy through exports, with handicrafts being one of the major export items of India.

Handicrafts are also an important part of India's tourism industry, with tourists visiting the country specifically to purchase handicrafts and experience the country's rich cultural heritage.

In addition, Handicrafts have a great impact on the environment, most of the traditional handicrafts are eco-friendly, using natural materials and techniques that have been passed down for generations, which are sustainable and do not cause harm to the environment.

Handicrafts play an important role in Indian society and culture. They are an important part of India's cultural heritage, an expression of the country's diverse cultural and regional identities, a medium of storytelling, an important source of livelihood and a great contributor to the economy. They are also an important part of India's tourism industry and an eco-friendly approach to the environment.

"Handicrafts are the heart and soul of Indian culture and tradition, and they must be protected and promoted for future generations to enjoy."

- S. Jaishankar

ଌ

XII

Contemporary Indian Handicrafts and Design

Contemporary Indian handicrafts and design refer to the modern interpretation and reinterpretation of traditional Indian handicraft techniques and motifs. This approach combines traditional craftsmanship with contemporary design elements to create unique and innovative products that appeal to a modern audience.

Contemporary Indian handicrafts and design can be seen in a variety of products such as home decor, fashion, and accessories. For example, a traditional hand-woven textile might be combined with modern geometric patterns and bold colors to create a unique and contemporary product. Similarly, traditional metalworking techniques might be used to create contemporary jewelry designs that incorporate modern shapes and finishes.

Contemporary Indian handicrafts and design are also influenced by global trends and styles, creating a fusion of traditional and modern elements. This approach not only preserves traditional techniques and motifs but also allows them to evolve and adapt to modern tastes and preferences.

Contemporary Indian handicrafts and design is also a way to increase the accessibility and affordability of traditional crafts. By incorporating modern design elements, these products can appeal to a wider audience, resulting in increased demand and a sustainable market for traditional crafts.

Contemporary Indian handicrafts and design is an approach that combines traditional craftsmanship with contemporary design elements to create unique and innovative products that appeal to a modern audience. This approach preserves traditional techniques and motifs while making them more accessible and affordable to a wider audience. It also allows traditional crafts to evolve and adapt to modern tastes and preferences, making them more relevant and sustainable in today's market. Additionally, the incorporation of global trends and styles in contemporary Indian handicrafts and design creates a fusion of traditional and modern elements, which adds to the diversity and richness of Indian handicrafts.

"Indian traditional art and craft is a window to the country's rich cultural heritage and it must be preserved and promoted for future generations to appreciate."

- Piyush Goyal

ꙮ

XIII

The Export of Indian Handicrafts and its impact

The export of Indian handicrafts has had a significant impact on the country's economy and society. Handicrafts are one of the major export items of India and have played a crucial role in the country's economic development.

Handicrafts exports contribute significantly to the country's foreign exchange earnings, providing a vital source of income for the government. It also creates employment opportunities for a large number of people, particularly in rural and remote areas where traditional crafts are an important source of livelihood. Additionally, exporting handicrafts help to promote Indian culture and heritage to the world.

The export of Indian handicrafts also has a positive impact

on the environment as most of the traditional handicrafts are eco-friendly, using natural materials and techniques that have been passed down for generations, which are sustainable and do not cause harm to the environment.

However, the export of Indian handicrafts also has its challenges. The industry is often unorganized and lacks standardization, which can result in poor quality products and inconsistent pricing. Additionally, competition from cheaper mass-produced goods can also negatively impact the market for traditional handicrafts.

The export of Indian handicrafts has had a significant impact on the country's economy and society. It provides a vital source of income for the government and creates employment opportunities for a large number of people. Additionally, it promotes Indian culture and heritage to the world and eco-friendly approach to the environment. However, the industry also faces challenges such as lack of standardization and competition from cheaper mass-produced goods.

"Handicrafts are not only a means of livelihood for artisans but also a reflection of India's rich cultural heritage."

- Rajnath Singh

❧

XIV

The Conservation and Revival of Indian Handicrafts

The conservation and revival of Indian handicrafts is an important aspect of preserving and promoting the country's rich cultural heritage. It involves efforts to protect and promote traditional craft techniques, motifs, and designs, as well as to support the artisans and communities who create them.

One of the key ways in which Indian handicrafts are being conserved and revived is through government-led initiatives. The government provides financial assistance and training to artisans and craftspeople, to help them improve their skills and market their products. There are also efforts to promote traditional crafts through cultural festivals and exhibitions, as well as through the establishment of craft museums and cultural centers.

NGOs and non-profit organizations also play an important role in the conservation and revival of Indian handicrafts. They provide training and support to artisans and craftspeople, as well as promote traditional crafts through education and awareness-raising campaigns. Additionally, they work to increase the market for traditional crafts by connecting artisans with buyers and promoting the use of traditional crafts in interior design and fashion.

Private sector also plays a significant role in the conservation and revival of Indian handicrafts. Many companies are working to promote traditional crafts by incorporating them into their products and design. This helps to increase the market for traditional crafts and provide a sustainable source of income for artisans and craftspeople.

The conservation and revival of Indian handicrafts is an important aspect of preserving and promoting the country's rich cultural heritage. It involves efforts to protect and promote traditional craft techniques, motifs, and designs, as well as to support the artisans and communities who create them. The government, NGOs, non-profit organizations, and private sectors all play an important role in this effort through providing financial assistance, training, promotion, education and awareness-raising campaigns and connecting artisans with buyers.

Indian handicrafts have a rich history and cultural significance that dates back to ancient times. They are an important part of India's cultural heritage and are deeply rooted in the country's rich history and traditions.

Handicrafts are an expression of the country's diverse cultural, ethnic, and regional identities and are a reflection of the lifestyle, customs, and traditions of the communities that create them.

"The beauty of Indian traditional art and craft lies in its diversity and the way it reflects the country's rich cultural heritage."

- Nirmala Sitharaman

ဢ

XV

Conclusion: The ongoing relevance and significance of Indian Handicrafts.

Handicrafts also play a significant economic role in India. They provide employment opportunities for a large number of people, particularly in rural and remote areas, where traditional crafts are an important source of livelihood. They also contribute to the country's economy through exports, with handicrafts being one of the major export items of India.

However, traditional crafts are also facing challenges such as competition from cheaper mass-produced goods and lack of standardization. Therefore, the conservation and revival of Indian handicrafts is an important aspect of preserving and promoting the country's rich cultural heritage.

Despite these challenges, the ongoing relevance and significance of Indian handicrafts cannot be denied. They continue to be widely practiced today, and the demand for traditional crafts is growing. Contemporary Indian handicrafts and design approach is also being adopted which combines traditional craftsmanship with contemporary design elements to create unique and innovative products that appeal to a modern audience.

Indian handicrafts are an important part of India's cultural heritage and continue to play a significant role in the country's economy and society. They serve as a medium of storytelling, depicting the myths, legends, and daily life of the people and are an eco-friendly approach to the environment. It's important to continue to support traditional crafts and artisans in order to preserve and promote this rich cultural heritage for future generations.

OTHER BOOKS OF THE AUTHOR

1. The Moments When I Met God
2. Kashiyile Theertha Pathangal
3. GURU GYAN VANI
4. Abhiprerak Gita
5. ASSI SE JAIN GHAT TAK
6. Hopelessness of Arjuna
7. The Soul and It's True Nature
8. Sense of Action (Karma)
9. Action through Wisdom
10. Action through Wisdom
11. THEORY AND PRACTICAL OF EVERY ACTION
12. LOGICAL UNDERSTANDING OF THE SUPREME
13. THE IMPERISHABLE SUPREME
14. Yatra Nishadraj se Hanuman Ghat Tak
15. Yatra Karnatak Ghat se Raja Ghat Tak
16. Yatra Pandey Ghat se Prayagraj Ghat Tak
17. Yatra Ranjendra Prasad Ghat se Dattatreya Ghat Tak
18. YaatraSindhiya Ghat se Gwaliar Ghat Tak
19. Yatra Mangala Gauri Ghat se Hanuman Gadhi Ghat Tak
20. Yatra Gaay Ghat Se Nishad Ghat Tak
21. MAA GANGA, GHATEN EVM UTSAV
22. Ganga Arti Dev Deepavali evam Any Utsav
23. Potentials of Digitalized India
24. VEDIC CONSCIOUSNESS
25. A Brief Introduction to Vedic Science
26. Kashi ke Barah Jyotirling
27. IMPACT OF MOTIVATION
28. Let's have a Milky Way Journey
29. Color Therapy in a Nutshell

30. Rigveda in a Nutshell
31. Yajurveda in a Nutshell
32. Samveda in a Nutshell
33. Atharva Veda in a Nutshell
34. Ayushman Bhava - Ayurveda
35. Srimad Bhagavad Gita and Upanishad Connection
36. Srimad Bhagavad Gita - an attempt to summarize each chapter.
37. Facts and Impact of Nakshatra
38. Astro Gems - NAVARATNA
39. Ekadashi - A Concise Overview
40. A Concise View of Hanuman Chalisa
41. Inspirational Gita
42. Nakshatraranyam
43. Summary of 18 Mahapuranas
44. Synopsis of 18 Upa Puranas
45. Rigvediya Upanishads
46. Shukla Yajurvediya Upanishads
47. Krishna Yajurvediya Upanishads
48. Samavediya Upanishads
49. Atharvavediya Upanishads
50. The Seven Great Sages
51. From Rocket Scientist to President Dr. APJ Abdul Kalam
52. The Visionary's Voice - Quotes of Dr. APJ Abdul Kalam
53. The Wisdom of Swami Vivekananda: Insights and Inspiration from a Legendary Spiritual Teacher
54. Ayurvedic Remedies from the Garden
55. Sages and Seers
56. Rising Strong – Motivational Stories of Women
57. Beyond Flames -Mystery stories of Funeral Ghat Manikarnika
58. The Origins of Tulsi: A Look at the Mythological Roots of the Plant"

59. The Holistic Cow: A Look at the Physical, Spiritual, and Cultural Importance of Cows in India
60. Arts of Healing
61. Exploring the Divine
62. Understanding Five Elements
63. The Etymology of Ram
64. Symbols of India
65. Voice of Change (About Speeches of Great Men)
66. She Speaks (About Speeches of Great Women)
67. Patriotism on Celluloid – Brief About Patriotic Films
68. The Music of Motivation: A Brief Guide to Inspirational Film Songs
69. **Unlocking the Secrets of the Dashopanishads**
70. A Cultural Mosaic
71. Ancient Traditions, Modern Minds
72. Ecos of Ancient Wisdom
73. Beneath the Surface
74. From Temples to Ashrams
75. Sages of the Subcontinent
76. The Art of Healling (Ayurveda, Yoga & Naturopathy)
77. Indian Kitchen
78. The Festivals of India
79. The Indian Epics Retold
80. The Power of Mantras
81. The Indian River Ganges
82. The Indian Architecture
83. Rites of Passage
84. The Indian Silk Road
85. The Indian Literature
86. The Indian Villages
87. The Indian Folks & Crafts
88. The Way of Buddha
89. The Ramayan of Tulsidas

90. Astrological Remedies
91. The Secret Power of Motivation
92. Secret of Developing your Inner Strength
93. The Secret Path to Motivation
94. The Art and Secret of Positive Thinking
95. The Secrets of Practicing Ethical Living
96. Indian Art and Painting
97. The Indian Herbalism
98. Bharatanatyam to Kathak
99. Exploring India's Astrological Remedies
100. The Indian Festival of Flowers
101. Indian Handicrafts

CONTACT

DR. JAGADEESH PILLAI

PhD in Vedic Science

Four Times Guinness World Record Holder

Winner of Mahatma Gandhi Vishwa Shanti Puraskar and Global Peace Ambassador

Gemology, Astro & Vastu Consultant - Spiritual Counselor

Consultant for designing World Record Ideas

Efficient Tarot Card Reader

9839093003

myrichindia@gmail.com

drjagadeeshpillai@facebook

drjagadeeshpillai@instagram

jagadeeshpillai@youtube

www. JAGADEESHPILLAI.com

|| LOKAHA SAMASTHAHA SUKHINO BHAVANTU ||

Printed by Libri Plureos GmbH in Hamburg,
Germany